The Fire in Their Eyes

The Fire in Their Eyes

Spiritual Mentors for the Christian Life

GREGORY MICHAEL SMITH

PAULIST PRESS **NEW YORK/RAMSEY**

NIHIL OBSTAT:
Thomas J. Driscoll, S.T.L.
Censor Librorum

IMPRIMATUR:
+ Most Rev. Walter W. Curtis, S.T.D.
Bishop of Bridgeport
September 30, 1983

The Nihil Obstat and Imprimatur are official declarations that a book or pamphlet is free of doctrinal or moral error. No implication is contained therein that those who have granted the Nihil Obstat and Imprimatur agree with the contents, opinions or statements expressed.

Cover design and interior art by Walter Hearn.

Library of Congress
Catalog Card Number: 83-62951

ISBN: 0-8091-2620-6

Published by Paulist Press
545 Island Road, Ramsey, N.J. 07446

Printed and bound in the
United States of America

Contents

Acknowledgement

No accomplishment however small is the work of an individual person. This book has come into print because many caring persons have found its concept meaningful. Personal thanks are due to all those who, in any way, shared their life stories so that the basic premise of the book would be sound. Thanks also to James Emswiler of Silver-Burdett and Jean Marie Hiesberger of Paulist Press whose professional support and editorial comment made this work complete. Special gratitude is due to Patricia Bruhin whose impeccable typing made this manuscript readable. Lastly to my bishop, Walter W. Curtis, whose mentoring has been witnessed in the encouragement of my writing and in the generosity of time given to produce such manuscripts.

Dedication

To the best of
all mentors:
My Mother, Father and Aunt.

In Memory
of
Mary Kate McFarland

Foreword

One of the world's highest railway lines via steam locomotive winds through the Andes Mountains from Lima, Peru to La Paz, Bolivia. The trip begins near the playa and climbs to Cuzco in the antiplano, high amidst clouded peaks and ruins of Machu Picchu. Reaching the Bolivian border at Lake Titicaca, passengers disembark to conclude the trip by steamship and rail to La Paz. Up the treacherous incline the six-car train pauses intermittently at native villages, adding stronger steam engines.

The Andes train ride might be a modern parable for our spiritual life. As each engine gives new, stronger purpose to the train, our lives pick up specific energies to assist us in reaching spiritual maturity. Some of these energies are self-discovered, as in learning from our market events. Others come from people—mentors who walk with us, giving guidance for our journey. The remainder are energies from God—his grace. God gives us his life so that we may have the momentum to pursue ongoing conversion. The analogy finds theological underpinnings in a sermon of Meister Eckhart. Eckhart's allegory is about creation and incarnation:

> The shell must be cracked apart if what is in it is to come out, for if you want the kernel you must break the shell. And therefore if you want to discover nature's nakedness you must destroy its symbols, and the farther you get in,

the nearer you come to its essence. When you come to the One that gathers all things up into itself, there you must stay (Sermon, "Honor Thy Father").

Eckhart's insights capture the symbolism of brokenness, offered as a means to wholeness. We come to terms with our brokenness as we learn we are valued and loved. Jesus, our incarnational symbol, brings to our consciousness a new plan for living. By becoming like us he entitles us to claim God as our own. Jesus shows us a God who loves us and allows us to possess him. Out of Jesus' brokenness we learn how to be open to love. In appreciating Christ's death, we catch a glimpse of why brokenness opens up the possibility of new life.

The modern-day parable *Hinds Feet on High Places* by Hannah Hurnard captures some of the intensity of the spiritual passage. Hurnard's main character must discern good spirits from bad; she must also learn to trust in the Lord. The hardest part is in understanding that the Lord doesn't stop our falls; rather he always picks us up.

The saga of adult life records the need to rework our lives as we face the challenge of new consciousness. Reconciliation is elemental here. Doris Donnelly (*Learning To Forgive*) considers personal reconciliation absolutely essential for self-definition and the resolution of spiritual inertia. Pain, growth, giving up and taking on—all those elements of change—become features which can turn us around to new spiritual lives. Reconciliation helps us divest ourselves of our hurting ways so that we can learn new healing ways. The healing of our spiritual lives begins when we learn to swallow our pride, accepting ourselves as fallen and in need of repair.

How one passes through the adult years has great bearing on spiritual maturation. This is not to say that adult tansitions are smooth. They are often traumatic and painful. The quality of adult transition is weighed by how well one accepts change, accedes to new direction and grows up to its standards. Accordingly, the spiritual life deepens as one becomes freed from adolescent selfism. When one no longer needs to play god, it is time to let God into one's life.

When we were young adults we were impatient, desiring to conquer the world. But as the middle years approach, there's need to reappraise earlier expectations in the light of the already achieved, the never to be achieved and the not really worth achieving. It's not unusual to doubt personal worth. It's part of growing up adult. The new consciousness of adulthood can create major problems as well as cure some. Maturity occurs when we realize that, in perspective, life's ambitions, realized or unrealizable, are not as important as well-being, integrity and peace. However, these are difficult years—years which must be accompanied by an increasing awareness of the implications of the Gospel. Often Gospel implications were never clearly understood in our youth; in the adult years they can be made strong and clear. Falling from the false assumptions of our positions is a revolutionary experience. It tells a tale—a story of how limited we are, but also naive, and understandably untested and undeveloped. Adulthood demands grown-up responses. But spiritual maturity is all about our stories of weakness, vulnerabilities and longing to be forgiven. When we learn to forgive our own lapses we begin a new chapter in our story. It's in adulthood where true, deep and meaningful faith should occur. Only an adult can take on a responsible faith commitment. As we critique our life experiences, sorting them out, we can pull from them newer and deeper meanings of life. When we are flat on our backs at the bottom of the wall, there is little left but somber reflections on what used to be—and what will be from now on.

After giving a talk in a New Jersey parish a few years ago, a woman participant came forward to express thanks for having had the opportunity to share spiritual insights. In the course of that one-time-only conversation, I asked her to describe to me what my presentation had meant for her. Quite unabashedly she stated, "Oh, your thoughts were another stone to help me cross the river of life!"

Stepping stones, steam engines, mentors, spiritual energies, new consciousness—all are valuable when they assist us in becoming more dependent on God. But believe me, becoming spiritually dependent takes guts. The holy life calls for the kind of adult maturity which eventually turns religiously weak people into loving mentors and spiritual guides. Spiritual mentors serve no more than levers helping us assume spiritual positions in our lives needed to grow more deeply in touch with the Lord. "Love others as I have loved you," is the mentoring principle. We might conclude that when one becomes a spiritual mentor, one has learned personal healing and so can be for others what others have been for them.

Introduction

This little book attempts to accomplish one goal: to discover the influence of spiritual mentors on people's lives.

This author has reason to believe that many people fail to take charge of their spiritual potential because they lack motivation and focus. For many no spiritual focus is perceived as meaningful or realizable. And so the years are lived stagnantly, empty of energized spiritual movement. For others more sense is made out of adult life precisely because a spiritual direction is established. Why does spiritual potential go dry in some people while others embrace challenges almost gleefully? Why do some stick with a childhood appreciation of spirituality, while others move on to great transcendent heights?

Synthesizing the research data accumulated over the past few years regarding adult conversion, one element seems consistent with people's discovery of new religious potential. That single constant factor is best described as the presence of a facilitating person. A facilitating person is one who can act as a spiritual mentor or guide. This, then, will be the issue addressed in these pages. Attendant to our discussion will be applications to the recently restored *Rite of Christian Initiation of Adults*. The adult catechumenate specifically revives the role of the spiritual mentor or guide in sponsors, personal and communal.

Our culture complicates one's search for a spiritual guide. Modern day America offers us few heroes and heroines to emulate. So intense is the American love of individualism that few adults are stalwart enough to stand against that cultural whirlwind. And so Americans learn quickly enough that if you're going to make it, you'd better do it yourself. Furthermore, wisdom and insight, once society's affirmation of old age, are relegated to science, thus leaving untouched a massive emotional vacuum in our lives. And yet scanning the literature of science and industry, the evidence is clear. Those who succeed have had mentors. Our approach here will be to draw conclusions from this literature and apply it to the spiritual domain of life.

Needless to say, we need to affirm the place of spiritual guides in our lives. We must goad our modern culture into fostering and affirming mentorship. No one will have a life of quality without the gift of accumulated wisdom and virtue from good people. People we can look up to! Mentors! Spiritual guides to assist our growth, so that in turn we might do the same for others.

In these pages the role and vitality of the spiritual mentor will be discussed. It will be our goal to demonstrate the significance of the spiritual mentor as a sponsor to spiritual maturity of the already baptized as well as for the yet-to-be initiated into the faith. Hopefully, once illustrated, some of us may realize our own unique mentoring gifts and offer them, as well as be open to the gifts and insights of others.

Many people affected my life significantly. All were my mentors. Some challenged; some chastised; others affirmed. Not all were men; in fact many were women. Blessed by years in the presence of dominant self-assured women I grew up with more a sense of emotion and imagination than reason and logic, although these are also part of my gifts. My male mentors are singular and few; the women are numerous and composite. In respect to them all my grandmother will be their stand-in.

Recalling Old Truths

I.

Recalling Old Truths

LOOKING BACK

In the 1950's a person seldom asked the question, "Can anyone give me advice?" If you were below twenty-one you were expected to find wisdom and sound advice in your superiors—parents, teachers and clergy.

Minding your adults was a universal standard in those days. Adults were expected to have the important answers about life as well as the virtue to prove it in action.

As I think back on it, my formative years were influenced less by peers and more by the adults who nurtured and protected me. Reflecting on these receding memories I'm humored by the seemingly simple process of growing up then. This judgment, of course, is based upon a comparison with the apparent complexity of growing up in today's world.

Thirty or more years ago my peers and I never thought of questioning or challenging the adults—and if we did we kept it secret to ourselves. Don't get me wrong. We didn't buy all their opinions just because they were adults, but mostly because they were adults whom we respected.

In simpler times, it was relatively easy for boys to find adult men as heroes. Sports idols, teachers and firemen figured in easily. They all had one thing in common—they publicly gave witness to self-sacrifice and dedication, regardless of salary. And we were awed by them. Growing up for us meant growing up to be like them.

There were also heroines for young women to emulate. The girl of yesteryear was more docile than today's female. In the limitations of the times, adult women showed courage and timeless dedication to the girls challenging them on to motherhood, education and nursing.

And then there were all those movie stars—bigger than life but just this side of fantasy, and not yet, in today's sense, letting it all hang out. We were impressed by them because they had "class." They set a standard.

LOOKING FOR ADVICE

Years ago a young person knew where to go for advice. If your parents didn't know the answer, certainly the teacher did, as well as the local pastor. And advice they had to give out, carte-blanche. They fulfilled their roles by passing on the wisdom imparted to them. And except for sex—it seems every generation learns this in other-than-mentoring-ways—we accepted their advice, sometimes unquestioningly.

Adults in those days knew where to turn for help. It was a stubborn person who would not accept the advice of the pastor, the policeman, or the doctor. We may counter today, claiming that some pastors, policemen and doctors led us down the rosy path but at that time and in that cultural setting the pieces seemed to fit.

I recall patiently waiting for the chancellor of our diocese to decide whether I should go on to the seminary or not. It would never have dawned on me to question his authority or his wisdom. Today I might have handled this differently. It was his duty to appraise the situation and decide on my future. Having little experience in life I knew instinctively that I wasn't expected to make these kinds of decisions. They were not mine to make, at least not yet. And it was comforting not to be rushed into adulthood.

The days before Vatican II were quiet times for many lay people. Only a privileged few knew the errors and inadequacies of our ways. And because religious leaders were held in such awe and respect it was easy to transfer our spiritual decisions over to them.

My mother would often tell me that my pastor knew what was right and I'd better listen. Today I know that she really thought differently in private but bowed to what was at the time socially acceptable. Whether from the sisters in the school or fathers in the rectory, advice was free for the asking. We expected the nuns and priests to have all our spiritual problems neatly worked out. All you had to do was ask—and the answers were there.

RESPECTING OTHERS

These old scenarios impart facts very essential about life—primarily that adult-child relationships were more defined then than today. Young and old knew each other's domains and therefore could respect each other's privileges. On one hand, being a child guaranteed you protection from the demands of serious decision making, while, on the other hand, being an adult gave you a willing audience.

Today I'm constantly amazed at how priests looked upon older priests in years gone by. There was respect and admiration unsurpassed by any fraternity today. The venerable pastors of today retell their dependence upon the older men of yesteryear to give them guidance in their novice phase of ministry. The newly ordained looked up to a senior curate or pastor; one deferred to a monsignor. And this wasn't just clerical folderol! The older men felt obliged in conscience to instruct and direct the younger men. The younger men correspondingly were duty bound to listen and learn. Today's clerical relationships are peer relationships built less on master-novice relationships and more on personal ones. Something old is lost; something new is gained.

This same respect existed between married couples and their in-laws. Mother-in-law jokes aside, many young couples thrived because they could depend upon the wisdom of the older in-laws whose own marriage was an archetype to theirs. Some today comment that socio-economic conditions are forcing older and younger couples once again to occupy the same household. If so, in some ways, the old virtues will surface once more.

PERSON TO PERSON SUPPORT

There seems to be no substituting for person to person support. The old chauvinistic maxim that "behind every great man is a woman" may not be far from the mark once we extrapolate it from its sexist underpinnings. People become great for three reasons: (1) they possess potential greatness; (2) they realize their potential; (3) someone helps them see the reasons for becoming great. Wisdom is passed on, not earned or learned. The role of the spiritual guide is less one of information collector and more one of interpreter of life. The mentor is not to give answers but to listen to questions.

The old days were not necessarily better days. My reference to them only marks an historical context in which certain components of human interchange were more distinct than today.

THE SPIRITUAL GUIDE

A markedly absent component in today's culture is the role of the spiritual guide. Why? Common sense alone tells us that the anti-hero/heroine stereotype still reigns supreme. Modern though we be we are still unabashedly naive when it comes to human motivation. Rather than provide prototypes for our emulation we disdain them, choosing instead to find skeletons in each other's closets. The price we pay for so-called honesty in institutions does less to correct these same bastions and more to diminish the possibilities of learning from these environments. We seem to be two-faced, preferring heirlooms in our living quarters, and ersatz in our lives.

Having learned that nothing succeeds like success we correspondingly forget that everything tires without trust.

Getting on with a life which manages to attain a degree of sensitiveness to spiritual values demands guidance. A virtuous person will not become virtuous if few are virtuous. God's grace notwithstanding, we need to see in each other the successful resolution about becoming good people.

I think more often these days about those who so admirably provided me with the motivation and challenge to do right with my life. In every case these adults demonstrated certain qualities about life and staunchly witnessed their faith. While they were able to introduce me to a newer understanding of human life they were also able to assist my spiritual growth.

REFLECTIONS

Two people come to mind concerning my adolescence. The first and foremost was my maternal grandmother. Mary Kate was able to interpret the subtle challenges my parents placed before me and as if with magic made them more palatable and exciting and less threatening. Her resounding words were always a gentle reminder: "Don't let them get you down!" Although she never explained who "they" were, I guessed that her caution was less about people and more about an attitude about myself. I sometimes think she may have had a clue to the inner workings of the spiritual life. Our "getting down" doesn't come from others but from the demons of depression within us.

My grandmother believed totally in me. Whatever I accomplished was good, but more importantly she showed me that what I did was not as important as what I was. And her insights have stuck until now. Her mentoring was a gift of love. I retain no voluminous record of her insights or philosophical ramblings, but I live in her faith and trust. Her belief in me made it possible for me to believe in others.

Surprisingly the other adult who also takes a central place in my growing years was neither a family member nor a Catholic. During adolescence and young adulthood I worked at a supermarket. It's here that, to my own mind, I encountered the good, the bad, and the ugly. Mostly it just was plain ugly! For some reason I remained eight years in that part-time employment precisely because the manager liked me—saw some quality in me which at that time I didn't recognize. Leonard spotted my potential. He knew he could never attain this for himself but he wanted it for me. And so he did his best to support my blossoming life and keep me out of harm's way. To this day, as I remember him, I can still feel the warmth of his pride in having a seminarian in his store. Doctrines and denominational loyalties had nothing to do with it. When he had to chastise me it was because he knew I could transcend the ugliness he had to bear day after day. And I flourished under his guidance.

After my ordination I entered a world where I was to be my own man. Again loving hands guided me through some turbulent days. A primary mentor in my novice years was a priest. Bill was one of those rare people who seemed to have an inside track into life. Fragile, vulnerable, and admittedly imperfect himself, he was able to find in me the potential for greatness. For years his guidance was subtle. But he was there. Periodically he would appear like a "Christmas—Future" to affirm, to jokingly correct and to challenge. I must say that today I hold him in highest respect not because he gave me insight but because he was lovingly concerned. In his usual tongue-in-check fashion, he once quipped before a group of priests after I had finished a lecture on the sacraments: "How did you come to this knowledge? I never taught you these things."

No one was as influential in my academic and professional life as Lee. Unsurpassed in virtuosity, Lee could enrapture his audience as he wove a cocoon of insight and wisdom. One came away from Lee's classes filled with vision, awed at life. Lee's brilliance overpowered me, but I mostly admired his inner self—wounded, less than successful, a Don Quixote at the windmill. I was glad that such fallen knights were still around. Lee coaxed the clerical pants right off me. He was no fool for the pedantic, the arrogant. He made me see, made me feel, that if I could learn to love life, people and God, I had accomplished what living was all about.

Even though some people haven't had mentors in their lives, they should have. Everyone needs them. Part of the maturing process to adulthood centers on finding life references in one's spiritual guides—one's mentors. In remembering their impact upon our lives we become sensitized to the fact that we are not self-sufficient little egos, but rather malleable clay in the hands of caring potters.

MENTORS IN THE CULTURAL CONTEXT

The point of all this is homey. We need each other. We need to find in one another trust and belief. This is all the more apparent today when our cultural milieu often encourages isolation and individualism rather than community and commitment. But we are not alone, and we need people to believe in us. Many people long to find someone who will believe in them but cannot. And so the results are market for newspaper copy: suicides, addiction, violence, insanity.

CONVERSION

The process of becoming Christian seems to have the ring of modern nuance to it. Actually diving deeply into one's need for transcendence is ageless. People have always come to conversion points in their lives. The depth or change asked at that moment could be accepted or postponed. In the case that conversion's call was embraced one met head-on a marker event in life. The method of helping adults come to terms with a transcendent Other in their lives, and specifically as expressed in Christian and Catholic terms, has had a diverse history. Earlier on an adult who desired intimacy with the Lord did so through penances and asceticism, sometimes culminating in formal monastic life. More often it involved an educational process which enculturated the novice into the social decorum and doctrines of the institutional Church. Regardless of method, converting adults usually recognized some significant person who introduced them into a new and far more meaningful appreciation of the spiritual life.

We tend to depreciate the narrow educational approach to conversion today. We understand change as less a reassessment of data and more an integrated evaluation of life and its destiny. In that context the restored adult catechumenate underwrites a basic principle: someone significantly sponsors us into God's life of faith. The specifically designated sponsor in adult conversion is neither educator nor aesthete. The sponsor is a believer who channels the grace of faith to the novice as a mediator for God. Quite simply the significant sponsor walks the novice through the avenues and roads of life's spiritual quest. In some cases this is immediate and action-related; in other cases it is long-term and intangible. The adult catechumenate provides a prototype whereby both the believing community as sponsor-mentor and the individual Christian as sponsor provide a basic sustenance to those significant times in life when getting to appreciate the need for transcendence is the key to maturity and salvation in the Lord.

BEING CHRISTIAN

This book assumes that we are more than human. We are also Christian. The paramount command of Jesus urges us to care for each other. St. Ignatius put it another way: "What have we done for Christ?" We might paraphrase this and ask: "What have we done for each other?"

In these few pages I have shared with you my indelible memories of mentors. I presume that you could also share equally rewarding stories about how significant people have shaped your life and your faith.

Our big concern in the following pages will be about the role of the spiritual mentor. By illustrating its importance, we will suggest that the role can once again be affirmed and utilized.

In the next chapter I will address myself to these questions: What is a mentor and what does a mentor do?

II.

What Is a Mentor?

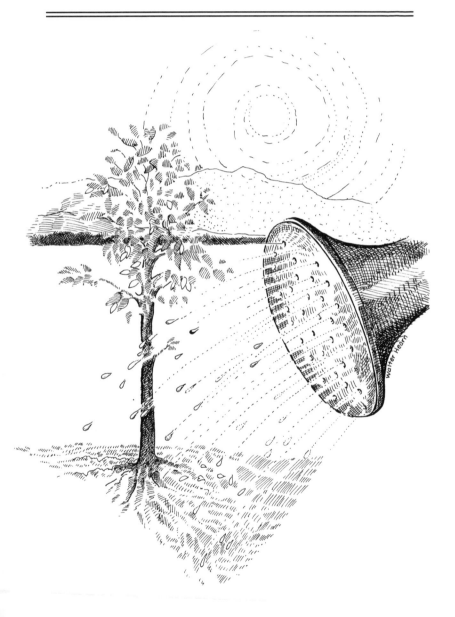

SIGNIFICANT INFLUENCES

In quite simple terms Alfred North Whitehead would understand life as being in the thick of things—present partnered to the past while anticipating the future. We need to become aware that who we are now has been conditioned by what we were when and will determine in some way what we will be later on. None of us has traveled this highway alone. In the last chapter examples were offered to illustrate how significant people have had impact on my life. Needless to say, everyone of us could share similar illustrations.

We all share in a basic human nature—the framework of being one of God's creatures. The width and quality of that experience is conditioned by personal choices, opportunities, education, and prevailing socio-economic environments. We can never be unpartnered in life; no matter how alone we might feel at a given moment, we are really tied to the phenomena around us. Touched by others and our world, in turn we touch them and their world. For the believing Christian God also plays a significant part in personal histories. God touches our lives with sustaining grace through the Spirit of Jesus.

MENTORS

There are, therefore, influences upon our lives—some welcomed and others uninvited. One of the most significant influences on our lives is the people with whom we live. Some provide us with the affirmation needed to survive soundly. Others join with us in pursuing common goals. But of all those who walk the beaten path of life with us, only one makes such an impact that the change redirects adult life—and that's a mentor. Mentors are our own Michelangelos, drawing out of primitive substance the greatness that lies beneath—hidden and untapped. Mentors exert an integrative power on us. Evoking all the best from our substance the mentor helps us come to new awareness of our life and helps us subsequently to make decisions which concretize our potential.

Interestingly, the role of mentor in most societies has had a distinguished history. Whenever a society affirmed wisdom, age and experience, persons so respected for their acuity in the arts and sciences were utilized to aid others not yet so mature. Contrarily whenever a society loathed age and wisdom it could not affirm the role of mentor.

TRANSITIONS

Transition aptly describes our present culture. The fact that so much of life is in flux complicates people's abilities to cope with the demands of transition. Many modern commentators are urging us to focus on the need to support each other in the complexity of shifting values. Transition, it seems, needs sponsoring—wherein the reason for re-establishing the role of mentor. The mentor becomes acceptable in our own time because there is value in someone walking us through the difficult transitions of life. Interestingly enough the Church's timing in restoring the adult catechumenate has been right on target. Throughout the nation pastoral leaders are confirming one fact over and over again: people are in spiritual transition and need sponsoring. One way of accomplishing this is to begin appreciating the importance of the mentor in all phases of life, whether as sponsor in the movement of conversion or as adapted for renewal and restoration of the faith.

In a transitional age the whole idea of mentorship is quite germane. Modern pressures cause conflict and stress. And lives are so compacted that future planning is difficult. We have access to more data but prize knowledge less; we can be more in control of life but have lost the sense of destiny. Mentorship in our present society can help take the desperation out of living with today's changes and difficulties.

Daniel Levinson in *The Seasons of a Man's Life* claims that adult males have had mentors who have assisted them beneficially through early adult transitions. In some cases these mentors have been wives as well as employers, friends and agents. A mentor, Levinson proposes, is a person whose greater experiences and seniority offer a praxis for guiding the uninitiated, the novice adult. Although Levinson's study deals exclusively with males he states that this in no way denies that women also have mentors. History, it seems, would recount that all people can have mentors, although cultural conditions may have provided women with fewer mentors than men.

WHAT IS A MENTOR?

And so what is a mentor? Generally speaking a mentor is a person whose greater life experiences, education or accomplishments provide leverage for the uninitiated, questioning or searching person in coming to terms with life as pertains to one's potential, relationships, occupation, philosophy, opportunities, education or socio-economic status. Tracing back the word "mentor," it finds its genesis not in philosophical circles, but in the actual account of the role in the great literature of the Greeks. Mentor, we are told, was the wise and faithful counselor of Odysseus and Telemachus. A mentor, it seems, had significance because it existentially made a lot of sense to a lot of people.

The role of the mentor is as varied as there are needs for mentors. A mentor may be a teacher—weighing data and theory with us; a guide—walking with us through life's inevitable struggles; a witness—illustrating to us values to be held dear; and a listener—gently supporting our dreams and expectations. Gail Sheehy in *Pathfinders* would concur. Her investigations have led her to believe that the happiest adults are those who have confronted change, had mentors upon whom to rely and conquered those transitions.

Mentors form relationships with us. And those relationships are like all other human relationships, including shared feelings and deep emotional ties. The value in mentorship is that the mentor provides the means to critique one's walk into adult life. When the walk is ended, a mentor's role may end. Sometimes it ends with difficulty and friction—as in the case of a spouse-mentor.

It seems to me that a mentor helps us develop a finely tuned sense of self-esteem. When we come to terms with the fact that it is good to be a human being, we can engage our potential. We may become the person we should become.

Mentors give us new eyes. We learn to see through their eyes—who we are, who others are. Proverbially a mentor helps us light a light for our lives so that we don't have to curse the darkness.

THE FIRE IN THEIR EYES

A mentor helps the child in us become father to the man. Aiding and abetting adulthood—that's a mentor's key role. A mentor believes almost insatiably in persons becoming mature. Enamored by the realm of possibilities for our species a mentor exudes excitement about life, its diversification and the maximalizing of potential. I assume this is why we are drawn to mentors. We see the fire in their eyes and catch on fire ourselves.

Is the role of mentor open to all? Can the average person assume such a position? Obviously these are pertinent questions. If one is to narrow the role of mentor to the ivory towers of the university or the olympic heights of government, there will be few acceptable in such august roles.

However, we aren't discussing these kinds of exceptional genuises here. In the ordinary life of average people the mentor will be pretty average too. Theoretically a mentor may be any human being—that is, if that human being prizes life above all else and believes that becoming mature is important. Being a mentor does not involve professional expertise or academic degree, although such might help. A mentor may be our parent or our spouse. But the closer the relationship the harder for the novice to leave the nest. A mentor will be a friend, at least for a time, as well as a confidant.

The Church states that a sponsor should be a practical Catholic. If I understand this correctly, a practical Catholic is one who ideally has integrated faith-as-fact with faith-as-life and brings to the role of sponsor a lived wisdom needed to assist the novice Christian. Obviously in many cases this is far from the fact. However in the catechumenate where discipline can be maintained the sponsor-mentor is supposed to know more about living and loving God than intellectualizing to God, even though this is not incompatible with the role.

A mentor is someone who cares. A mentor will have any occupation there is—even might be a hobo. Mentors may be any age—younger than or older than their novices. It's the mentor's experience and wisdom that counts—the ability to listen, challenge, and affirm—and some reach this before others less as the result of accumulated years and more by chance.

In the lifetime of the average adult mentors enter, play their part and retire. Without our second glance, many of them fade into the remote recesses of our minds to be forgotten and their efforts given little esteem. But all mentors, even those we most detest, have had a consequential impact on our lives. Because of them we are who we are today. It is important, at least in the sense of appreciating others' efforts in our service, that adults remember and appreciate the mentors of their lives. Why? Simply because these dedicated people have had some part in the historical event of our lives. They are part of our memory, our collective stories of becoming human.

Reflect on Joe Anderson's experience!

Joe was twenty-eight when he realized that his handicap, near total legal blindness, would stymie his life. Those were desperate days. He had always thought that some invention, a cure perhaps or a stroke of luck, would improve his state. Joe was greatly saddened by the fact that he would never have a life like his peers.

That was until Mr. Stewart entered his life. Joe had been working hard at his job as a coordinator of products at a chemical plant. He had learned to "feel" out flaws and imperfections in the product run. Mr. Stewart, newly appointed shop manager, took Joe under his wing. It wasn't a morbid thing. Stewart believed that Joe had some potential—certainly more than Joe thought he had. Mr. Stewart gave Joe time—time to learn new processes. He constantly challenged Joe to overcome his blindness. As if by magic Joe began to feel better about himself. He began to believe that even though blind his mind could picture goals and create ideas. Joe became aware that he was more than a sum total of images in his eyes. Mr. Stewart moved on to an executive position and he asked Joe to come with him as his administrative assistant. Joe said no! He had learned to be his own person—he had skill and would succeed, with or without Mr. Stewart.

The experience of Joe Anderson was a happy one. Joe learned that he could transcend his physical disability. Mr. Stewart played a dominant role in Joe's life. Facilitating a process of self-definition, Stewart aided Joe in making a bridge in his life—crossing from depreciation to appreciation of personal talents.

Lest we forget that some mentoring relationships end up disastrously we might reflect on the experience of Jack and Ed.

> Jack was a junior partner in the law firm of James and Bower. In his early years as a graduate lawyer he had developed a mentor relationship with Ed, a law student. Ed depended on Jack for support and introduction into the legal profession. Jack was more than happy to introduce Ed to his peers and clients. He was proud of Ed, and proud that Ed counted on him for advice.
>
> When Ed graduated from law school and passed the bar, Jack threw him a grand party, inviting all his friends, including those who would look favorably upon Ed's promise. Ed landed a fine job with a well respected firm through Jack's influence. In the first few years of their relationship as peers, Ed and Jack shared many experiences, even vacations together. More and more Jack learned to lean on Ed, his apprentice. It was not long before Ed, stretching his wings, began to surpass his mentor, Jack.
>
> Somewhat threatened, Jack tried to slow down Ed's progress—sometimes by intimidation, other times by jealous rages. Ed found himself in a quandary. He wanted to stay close to Jack but also wanted his own life. He felt suffocated. Whenever he succeeded, Jack grew more irritable.
>
> Ed knew he couldn't live this way and confronted Jack with the problem. Jack took offense and closed Ed out from his life. A real reconciliation has never been possible.

THE MEMORY OF MENTORS

Mentors are humans who have been gifted with an uncanny ability to direct us to our goals. This is not a learned or earned gift; it is infused. However, this ability does not retard emotional ties which can constrain and destroy. Ed experienced jealousy in his mentor. Jack just couldn't face the fact that Ed had to move on and be his own person. And so a relationship which had begun as an earnest and honest experience ended as a bitter and unreconciled one.

Keeping alive the memory of our mentors helps fan our fire of service to others less mature than we. After all, if we have been justly served by our mentors, in turn we should do the same for the novices who come our way. Partnered with valuing our mentors is reconciling the results to our lives. For some of us, a mentor may have provided just the right insight, affording us a chance to see new definition in our lives. And then they may have left us to our own determination. Still others may have walked with us, bolstering and challenging our deepening insightfulness about life.

Recently I received an unexpected letter from a young woman I had once known. Now in her early twenties, graduating from college and anticipating marriage, she wrote asking me to officiate at her wedding. I was surprised that after so many years of no contact she should have still found me important to her life. The significance, it seems, comes from the impact I had on her. She explained it this way: "You were the most open, believing and educated adult I ever knew; and you have influenced all my life."

Believe me, I never imagined that I could have had such an impact upon this young woman. To have been her silent spiritual mentor through all these years, even though she was never able to admit it until now, is somewhat baffling.

Sadly some mentors latch onto us when their mentoring is

finished. And so we have to separate ourselves from them—a difficult task by any calculation.

When we learn to treasure our mentors, precisely because they have made a significant contribution to our lives, we can also learn to forgive them. Healing memories about mentors possibly frees us to affirm their services to us and to allow them their weaknesses. In healing hurting memories about mentors we come to terms with our own limitations and as such learn to appreciate our fleeting but important part in the lives of those who are still our apprentices.

I believe that we need to affirm the place of mentors in our lives because they have given us the possibility of becoming the people we might not have become without them. Descriptions pale when one tries to isolate the specifics involved in that process. But we might find it helpful to summarize the event of being sponsored by a mentor. A mentor contributes greatly to those moments of expanded consciousness in our lives. At those times a mentor helps us with an "aha" illumination. This is the time when we no longer need someone to lead us to the truth but have integrated it into our lives to such a degree that it makes sense because we make sense. A mentor urges us on to lifetime decisions—decisions which will make us who we are to become, or break us. A mentor should be sensitive to our weak human condition, but also challenging us to look beyond, becoming mystical if need be, so as to act out our convictions. A mentor invites us into the drama of life, out of ethos and into pathos, stamping our individuality with comedy and tragedy.

THE NOVICE

A word about the novice may be in order. The person who is a novice, and therefore in need of a mentor, need not be chronologically young. Novice or apprentice as used here refers to the state of one's experience, depth, expertise, range and enculturation into the life process. One may, indeed, by eighteen have the depth expected only in later years, while someone else may be fifty and uninitiated into life. In many cases the novice will be a person who has yet to work out a new consciousness about life and its potential.

THE MENTOR SERVES ALL

Adults who become immersed in mentoring give themselves freely to the good of other adults. Some of these aspects are educational; many are not. The mentor will become involved with the novice at the level of greatest need. Since a few mature adults can possibly serve many novices as mentors, it is likely that they could provide services in the following ways.

Champion of Causes

I doubt if any adult who has suceeded in life has done so without another adult as an advocate. We need support. But more importantly we need someone who believes in us. A mentor will champon the cause of the novice. This role could probably embrace advocating those areas of life that are still prophetic and idealistic. But simultaneously the mentor must stand for those objectives which make life realizable and practical. In championing ideals for the novice the mentor makes a statement about life and destiny as seen in the context of the mentor's own life.

Arbitrator of Issues

Mentoring necessarily involves one in helping to score the choices made by the novice. Arbitration by the mentor means assisting the novice in sorting through the variables of life—the contradictions, the paradoxes—and finding reasonable principles to live by. The mentor faclitates a synthesis with the novice, helping bring to closure the novice's decisions about life.

Supporter of Means

Once the novice gets hold of the attitudinal change demanded in life, there may be some hesitancy on getting these thoughts into action. A mentor aids the novice here because there is need for help in the transition from thought to action. In this capacity a mentor will challenge the novice to take a stand on new consciousnesses, making them tangible by subsequent deeds. Together the mentor and novice appropriate the means whereby life may be fully lived.

Counselor of People

There is reason to believe that wise counsel, above all else, is essential in leading adults to full living. The mentor may be called upon for this advice. The mentor must know how to counsel as well as how to help the novice keep firm in the determination to pursue goals. The novice may need assistance in the psychological area. Since tensions in life may conflict with values found in living or may overwhelm or stymie the novice, the mentor will have to listen to these stories and either help resolve the issues or know where help can be obtained.

Educator in Life

All education is to lead to a deeper appreciation of life. A mentor may be asked to bring to the novice that data necessary for becoming better informed about life. The mentor will teach less by formal educational methods and more by informal sharing of the values in living, giving the novice glimpses into the grandeur of life's plan.

Shapiro, Haseltine and Rowe in their research identify the role of mentor by the relationship the mentor has with the novice. Their categories which are named under a patron system include peer pals, guides, sponsors, patrons and mentors. Each category describes a significant person and his or her impact upon the life and occupation of another individual. The greatest of these is the mentor who has an intense relationship with the novice as teacher and advocate.

As a postscript, I recently spoke with leaders of a parish catechumenate. Their experience with sponsor-mentors was explicity non-educational. The educational-catechetical dimension they left to catechists. Experience taught them that the catechumenate sponsor best served the novice in being able to listen and challenge, to share and enable, rather than to inform by way of fact and doctrine. In brief a sponsor-mentor was least of all an educator and mostly a counselor and supporter of transition. With some irony there is a lesson to be learned from Mario Puzo's classical example of the Godfather, a patron and figure of strength for his novices, that is corollary to our illustration here.

A QUESTION OF BALANCE

In every classic example of mentor-novice relationships, e.g., Socrates and Plato, Albert and Thomas, the role is given parameters by the pursuit of truth and justice. Primarily both mentor and novice have to recognize their qualities as well as limitations. A mentor must know when to challenge, to affirm, to prod. But a mentor must also realize when to draw back, to wait patiently, to allow failure. A novice on the other hand learns best from the mentor when the wisdom of the mentor is treasured for what it is—a praxis for experimentation. If the novice gets bogged down in the personality of the mentor the treasure of experience may be lost in false adulation.

A mentor needs to show balance of judgment. That is, a mentor must be able to distinguish between appropriate incentive given the novice and dictatorial control. The Henry Higgins of *My Fair Lady* fame is not a mentor-archetype. The Shaw character is more Svengalian than Socratic. A novice does not give up personal liberty and decision-making to the mentor. Quite the contrary, the mentor must desire that the novice become more adept at decision-making and indeed more independent of the mentor.

A mentor's role necessarily must cease. When the novice no longer needs the mentor, when the apprentice surpasses the master, the role of mentoring unalterably changes. A mentor's greatest reward is the safe transition of the novice from needing advice to being able to transmit advice. It is an educational process. The mentor who teaches will impart wisdom to the uninitiated so that once imparted it grows to full bloom in a new teacher and mentor. The table eventually turns, and when it does there are no longer a mentor and novice but two peers. As sometimes happens in life the former mentor may turn to the former novice and ask for help. And this is as it should be. When we are sensitized to who we are to become, we are disposed to the ever changing dimension of who others are to become also.

The human condition requires sponsoring. Ages of human interchange have substantiated that we do well when supported by those whose life experiences can help us grow to mature living.

Our present age craves for affirming experiences. Although the age also suffers from intransiency and loss of primal values, its very change needs proctoring and sponsoring. In this context mentors make sense.

In the next chapter we will draw the role of the mentor, as we have discussed in this chapter, into the context of Christianity. With a focus solidly rooted in the Gospel values, the spiritual mentor's role will become defined by the Christian journey.

III.

What Is a Spiritual Mentor?

In more formal times the sons and daughters of the rich were assigned mentors. It was the mentor's task to challenge the young person's innate creativity—to bring out the best results.

The same was true of the arts. The Church often was patron (mentor) of the great artists of the day. One need only study the history of the lives of the medieval/renaissance Popes to understand this role. Quite clearly a Church leader felt an obligation to inform and support fledgling artists in the pursuit of creativity in its highest forms.

There is no reason to doubt that the greatest of saints had their mentors too. More often they were learned theologians and preachers; still many were simple priests, confessors who could listen to the spiritual journey of their penitents. In another sense great saints were themselves mentors. With an ironic twist of fate, St. Catherine of Siena found herself as a mentor to the highest Church officials, even to the Pope.

One might conclude then that a spiritual mentor must be a trained theologian, an eminent spiritual thinker, at least an ordained cleric. This would be erroneous. Spiritual mentoring, as witnessed in the life of Thomas More, is definitely not the sacrosanct territory of the cleric. Rather the spiritual mentor, like the secular mentor, may come from either the highest or lowest ranks of people.

GIFTS OF THE SPIRIT

If we are to take the effects of the sacrament of confirmation seriously, the results of the gifts bestowed through confirmation can be witnessed in the role of the spiritual mentor. A

Christian mentor is one who espouses the values of the Lord Jesus, utilizing the gifts of the Spirit in a way that testifies to the sacrament's fruitfulness and consequently becomes instrumental, helping these gifts become operational in a confirmed novice. The gifts of the Spirit which particularly seem germane in the life of a spiritual mentor are understanding, knowledge, and counsel. Wisdom is also important to their role but it seems to be more infused than acquired and thereby outside the instrumentality of the mentor.

The gift of understanding applies itself to Christian destiny. The mentor, filled with grace, affirms life now and relates it to the supernatural life-to-come. Specifically, the novice catches a glimpse of the what-will-be through the insights of the mentor. The mentor does the work of the Spirit in the sense that life here is caught up in the context of life eternal.

The gift of knowledge pertains to the truths about God. The mentor draws an analogy about our heavenly Creator and directs it to the life of the novice. The information shared is more than data. Rather it is truth informed with conviction.

Lastly, the mentor provides counsel for the novice. Developing a scenario of the spiritual life for the novice, the mentor helps the novice recognize the need to grow and mature spiritually. The mentor also acts under the guidance of the Spirit in assisting the novice in coming to terms with life and accepting limitations.

There is no reason not to conclude that mentors as Christians take their rightful role from baptism. If we can assume that the gift of the Spirit is incipient from intitiation into Christianity, then each Christian confirms over and over again a responsibility to be a sponsor-mentor when the opportunity presents itself. Explicitly the role of sponsor-mentor in the catechumenal process affirms the change begun in baptism—a new orientation to be alive for the Lord—and confirms the gifts of the Spirit in practice.

ADULT MINISTRY

Largely mentoring is an adult ministry—ministry in the sense implied by Henry Simmons (*The Quiet Journey*) a few years ago. Simmons understands the adult life process as a steadily deepening awareness into our own limitations and thereby the need for transcendence.

Simmons' proposal invites mentors into the throes of adult ministering. If secular society recognizes mentoring as an apt vehicle for walking people into life, how much more are we as Christians to make the Emmaus walk with others? Using Simmons' categories the mentor is called to help adults with transitions: (1) outer concerns of life to inner concerns: aiding adults in seeing their process of change as a positive way to experiencing Jesus anew; (2) finding new tools for the new aspects of life: joining adults in their search so as to provide a sense of camaraderie; (3) reconciling the what was with the what is: helping adults to forgive their pasts, finding humor in overinflated dreams, and formulating new dreams; (4) purification: welcoming newly reconciled adults into a community of adults already reconciled to life and maturing in their spirituality.

THE GREAT THESIS

There is a drama in mentoring. The dramatic moment finds its scene from the recurring theme of the Synoptic Gospels. Aware that Jesus' mission is leading to ultimate tragedy the Synoptic writers train their sites on impending resurrection as the solace for living the Lord's way. But they never leave us naive to the price to be paid—crucifixion. Awareness, that which brings the novice from immaturity to maturity, intersects life, i.e., we cannot hold onto life because it brings death; salvation implies crucifixion.

The spiritual mentor must place before the novice the great questions of spiritual living. Spiritual mentors must challenge novices to be what they can be. This implies the following set of operating principles.

A. *Jesus invites all to embrace his Way. It is attractive and appealing.* The mentor helps the novice appreciate the call to be a disciple, based on Luke 5:1-11, the call of the first disciples. The mentor supports the novice's invitation to a life of grace, even walks with the novice the first few miles.

B. *Jesus' Way challenges the value system of the world. Followers can be torn between what the world affirms and what Jesus proposes.* The mentor watches and waits for the novice's deepening of response. The waters of spiritual maturity are being tested at this point. Sincere Christians must learn that they really have no life of their own. They are to Christen the world in which they live. This is the laboratory of life for the novice. The mentor points out to the novice the trail of the early disciples found in Luke 9:1-7, 9:51-62, 10:1-20. In each case the disciples learn to give in a little more to Jesus' mission.

C. *Experiencing the cost of discipleship, the novice draws conclusions, sees strengths, recognizes weaknesses.* The mentor listens and comments. Using John's Gospel (Jn 21:15-19) the mentor challenges the novice to be open to possibilities, to be in service, to be willing to risk life. Here the mentor allows the novice to move beyond their relationship so that the novice can become a mentor to others.

D. *Recognizing the truth in the Lord's Way the novice matures and takes an appropriate stand.* The mentor, as a peer now, enhances the newly matured Christian's self-esteem and challenges to be "a light of the world."

This is Pentecost for the newly matured Christian. A
time when what happens does so because it happens
from the heart based on conviction.

If mentors are to give us new eyes to see our spiritual potential they must do so in light of the Gospel. The process contained in these principles is Gospel-centered. It is also a
prolonged process—one requiring discipline and prayer from
both mentor and novice. Michael Crosby (*Spirituality of the
Beatitudes*) proposes that conversion to maturity involves us in
a circle of insight. A spiritual mentor helps us address the jar-
ring experiences of our lives with new questions and new reflections in order to come to new understanding and hope. A
spiritual mentor helps us find a new way of living.

I would propose that the great thesis might be admirably
adapted to the sponsor-mentor's role in the catechumenate
process. Understanding that process as leading to a general re-
orientation of the novice's moral life to compatibility with the
Lord's demands, the sponsor-mentor might reflect upon the
thesis as a spiritual insight into one's own personal life and as a
praxis of intervention for the life of the novice. I would advise
readers involved in the catechumenate process to reflect on the
following pages with this in mind.

John Shea in "Storytelling and Religious Identity" (*Chicago Studies,* Spring 1982) describes the spiritual mentor as a
storyteller, a synthesizer of people's stories. A spiritual mentor
helps the novice Christian critique life's experiences by asking
probing questions—e.g., What am I doing with my life? Why
am I doing it? What does Jesus offer for my life? How do the
two get together? What specific action flows from this exchange? With this in mind we can try defining what is a spiritual mentor. Again by way of experiences, i.e., by the action of
mentoring, this definition takes shape.

In the purely religious sphere a mentor is a person whose

deeper faith life and insightfulness provide spiritual passage
for the uninitiated, searching or questioning person in coming
to terms with self, others, destiny, salvation and God.

What does that mean? Andrew Greeley (*Religious Imagination*) finds mentoring essential to the transmission of the
Gospel message. Greeley supports the fact that a spiritual
mentor is the significant means for a novice's coming to religious conversion. Simply put, a spiritual mentor's own life experiences are catalytic to another's religious growth.

The spiritual mentor is a guide for the novice believer.
The image provided for us is found in the Emmaus story in St.
Luke's Gospel (Lk 24:13-35). Jesus walks with and listens to
two humans share their life-sagas. And after listening he edu-
cates, building upon the novices' religious experiences. Jesus
supports their dreams and provides a connection between the
present time of dialogue and the time to come. Lastly Jesus
provides a transparency—a view to what can be if only one believes—experienced in the breaking of the bread.

In times of spiritual transition a mentor can direct us to
the Emmaus model. The spiritual mentor stands in for the
Lord. Consequently a Christian mentor has to be a good
Christian—one who is known for walking in the Lord.

A spiritual mentor should be an adult already initiated
into virtue and informed about the faith. The spiritual mentor
is also a transitional figure who invites and welcomes the novice Christian into a religious journey.

A spiritual mentor proposes to the novice Christian that
full virtuous living is possible. Through the mentor the novice
perceives the Lord's Way.

NOT A CULTIC HERO

Spiritual mentors are never to give novices the impression
that they are to be believed in. Rather mentors are to impress

novices with the fact that it is the Lord in whom we place our trust. The novice must be able to see the Lord through the mentor. The mentor makes growing up into Christian maturity possible. But the mentor is not to become a cultic hero. A mentor's role may be short-lived, and, given the emotional involvement with the novice, the mentor must eventually break from the novice.

FUNCTIONS

The functions for the spiritual mentor are varied. The mentor may serve as a guide for young adults—supporting their individual growth but challenging it to conform to the Lord's Way. The mentor may also be useful in the *Rite of Christian Initiation of Adults* (RCIA). Much of the catechumenate is journey and process-centered. The mentor may be an asset in the period of inquiry as well as in the period of mystagogy.

The role of sponsor as mentor in the *Rite of Christian Initiation of Adults* could be specified in the following ways: (1) advocate of growth: enlisting the novice into the process of initiation and encouraging perseverance: (2) listener of needs: providing the novice with the chance to ventilate anxieties and concerns; aiding penetration into moral insightfulness; (3) prayer-partner: faithful watcher and waiter during long hours of change and conversion—placing needs in prayer before the Lord; (4) reconciler of issues: through praying and listening the mentor helps the novice come to decisions of depth, i.e., whether to enter fully into the way of the Lord; (5) witness of life: called to illustrate Christian life in action, the sponsor-mentor demonstrates this by personal action based on belief, not merely on the novice's need. In the mystagogical dimension the sponsor-mentor might celebrate with the novice the unfolding understanding of Catholic heritage and the aspects of the Creed which round out the newly initiated adult's Christian life. The sponsor-mentor is also the final interpreter of the nuances of Catholic life style.

In catechesis of the young a mentor may be helpful as one of the community's storytellers. In that capacity the mentor makes the connection between what has been and what will be. There is also much spiritual direction a mentor could provide. Many adults can be greatly benefited by finding one of their own willing to listen to them, connecting their experiences to the experience of being Christian.

Because mentors are themselves involved in their own religious education, they are personally challenged to be the best of all teachers, listeners and believers. Inasmuch as their lives are to be vehicles for the Lord they are entered into an adult process of conversion and reconciliation. In their own passage they provide a credible focus for others' faith.

THE SPIRITUAL MENTOR
AS ADULT RELIGIOUS EDUCATOR

Every educator knows that when a good relationship gets established between students and teacher, it is a mentoring one. A spiritual mentor can offer the means whereby identification can be made between religious data and the Christian life process. The spiritual mentor invites the novice to cross the bridge of decisions and take a new focus on life.

In the world of adult religious education the spiritual mentor can (1) affirm the experiences of the novice adult, (2) help the novice assess those experiences, (3) draw syntheses, and (4) provide new insights into the life-yet-to-come. Lastly the Christian mentor must go one step further—helping the novice Christian know the love and saving power of God.

Education in this sense becomes an incarnational spirituality. Facts become lived events, faith finds a community context, and witness forms a new story.

Spiritual mentors play a profound role in all the sacred writings. Understood properly as accounts of spiritual journeys, the Old and New Testaments construct scenarios vivid with mentor-novice relationships. Through the Scriptures we catch the array of those whose life and faith experiences lend not only to the wisdom of the community but play significant roles for the nation Israel, as God's own spokespeople. Since the Sacred Scriptures are the oral to written history of God and his people, the role of mentor facilitates people encountering the mystery which is before, behind and around them. John Shea (*Stories of Faith*) alludes to the fact that the spiritual, scriptural mentor helps people find the revelation of the mystery of God deep inside themselves. Mentors put us in sync with what is yet to come.

The sacred texts offer insight into the nature of spiritual growth through the role that key figures play in the course of salvation history. The rudimentary foundation of mentoring is laid by God himself. His role as parent, creator, friend and confidant is evident throughout the Books of Genesis and Exodus. Even upon the eclipse of that special relationship that Adam and Eve enjoyed with the Creator, God continued to listen, chastise and bless his wary children. Evidence abounds in the sagas about Cain and Abel, Noah, Abraham and Moses. Each one encounters the Creator as a companion on the road to spiritual responsibility. On life's roadway God's signposts point his people toward their destiny.

In 1 Samuel 3:1-18, we have the classic case of dual mentorship. Young Samuel under the tutelage of Eli is visited by

God who provides Samuel with insight into the fate of Israel. Eli is mentor to Samuel's visitation; he is Samuel's interpreter. God on the other hand draws Samuel into a deeper relationship, challenging him finally to become a servant for the nation.

We might also suggest that Saul was mentor to David. 1 Samuel 16:14-23 illustrates a relationship that may have served such a purpose. But as we know, Saul becomes jealous of David's prowess. The mentor in this case refuses to let the novice grow up. The dire consequences to this story can give us pause reflecting on the need to keep mentoring and emotions separated.

Again in 1 Kings 15:19-21, Elijah and Elisha establish a mentor-novice relationship. Ministering to one another Elisha learns the ways of a prophet so that in 2 Kings 2:9-14 he can assume Elijah's power as his own.

The New Testament is an excellent study of mentoring. Jesus is the mentor par excellence who draws people in transition to himself, challenging them to carry on his work as their own.

The relationship of Luke and Paul also provides interesting reflection. Luke serves Paul's needs, recording for us Paul's insights and distributing some of his letters. But Luke takes his mentor's spiritual genius one step further. Luke writes a Gospel and the record of the early Church, the Acts of the Apostles.

Lastly we might consider that there was a significant mentoring relationship between the holy man Simeon and Mary and Joseph. Luke's Gospel records this (Lk 2:25-35). Although, from what we know, it is a short-term relationship, Simeon provides Jesus' parents with a spiritual insight into God's plans. Mary and Joseph marvel at his words, but we might conclude that they were never again the same.

THE BLESSINGS

Blessings abound in being a spiritual mentor. Blessings come in the forms of awareness, a spiritual consciousness that one's life can be advantageous to others. More altruistic than utilitarian, a spiritual mentor is called into the service of others: a Samuel called out of the night to work in the noonday sun.

MARTY'S BLESSINGS

Marty knew that something in him attracted others. This both exhilarated and frightened him. Lying awake in the early morning hours he reflected on the course his life was taking. Marty sensed great peace. New vistas were opening for him, new opportunities. Yet the greatest joy of all was seeing others sparked and challenged into newness of endeavor—growing closer to the Lord.

Marty was personnel director for one of the Fortune 500 companies. People were his business. But, more than that, he loved to help them grow to new heights, seeing things in newer ways than before, learning to care more about themselves and others. Marty couldn't describe what qualities others emulated in him but he knew that something happened. He prayed that he would never desire others to adulate him, but rather that they would become better people for themselves. He described his job as people's happiness, and happy people meant better business.

Marty's clients described him as "caring, supportive, interested in everyone's life." Marty's mentorship was a model of Christianity. His love of life made others want to live too. His gifts were the blessings of the Spirit. Marty didn't think of himself as an evangelist—he was markedly a non-dogmatic Christian—yet his attitude and actions sparked others to believe in God. Marty's life established one fact: the Lord was in his heart. And others wanted the same.

Blessings come too from affirming our mentors. Because some mentors are so gifted, their lives motivate and illuminate others' lives, and they are often remembered and quoted. Others affect people's lives significantly by thoughtfully sharing their spiritual experiences with candor and insight. Still many others are catalysts to new behavior.

Having mentors does not necessarily mean that one has the facility to speak about them. This is a unique gift too. Many people have difficulty expressing themselves in terms of their experiences; thus they speak rarely about their mentors, let alone write about them. They think that they do not have an adequate vocabulary to describe these significant events. One unused to storytelling, diary writing and journal keeping may be timid about sharing intimacies. Nevertheless mentors have been part of their lives.

A SURVEY

I surveyed fifty people who I believed had significant spiritual awakenings in their lives. This group of adults ranged in ages from twenty-eight to sixty-five. The sample group was composed of lay people (married, single, widowed, divorced, parents), clergy and religious. Their occupations were as diverse as any given population: engineers to educators, homekeepers to health care administrators, counselors to cleaning service personnel.

Their stories, samples of which are reported in the pages that follow, recall remembrances of significant people in their lives. In their own words intimate details about their spiritual growth emerge.

What results did I obtain? First and most interesting was the number of adults who reported that they had more than one spiritual mentor. Each mentor fit into a specific transitional period in their lives. The mentor-novice relationship was often short-term but significant. When the relationship ended the novice moved on to other needs with deeper maturity. Those attesting to more than one mentor commented that each mentor fit a stage in their lives, each becoming the more significant mentor. Second, those who were reluctant to share a story were willing to admit that they did have spiritual mentors. Third, there seems to be little correlation between the age and sex of the novice and the mentor. Rather, the novice chooses the person most apt to present spiritual needs. Fourth, many reported that their mentors were part of a continuum, i.e., one followed another in sequence. These novices perceived growth as a journey in which someone is needed constantly and consistently to guide. Lastly, many noted that their mentors were also their spiritual directors.

THE GIFT OF TELLING ONE'S STORY

The following ten stories form a composite representation of the responses to the survey. Although each story had nuances indicative of the unique history of each individual, these ten samplings preserve the quality while shortening the similarities.

A. Joe, an administrator, tells a story about Bob. At the time Bob served Joe as mentor, he was forty, a priest and social worker; Joe was nineteen.

At nineteen I was working in a summer poverty program in an inner city neighborhood. I experienced the basic needs of these people, their dissatisfaction and frustrations with life and society, as well as the challenge of the Gospel to speak to their daily lives. I personally experienced the results of these frustrations in violence and fires in city-wide riot disturbances. Amidst these turmoils and my own youthful inexperience, I needed to know and observe someone whose mature faith experience had a broader perspective. Bob was a person who had labored with these people for a number of years and had successfully communicated compassion through his daily living as well as planning successful programs. A few years later, I saw and heard him in a different context with middle class people. His gifts of understanding and listening to individuals and his ability to make the incarnation a reality in people's lives continued to inspire me. His words and actions clarified my own priorities.

Since then, our ways have parted. But his words and actions continue to impact my spiritual journey. In retrospect, his acceptance of his own sinfulness, his fidelity and his courageous compassion in the face of frustrating situations were key elements that communicated to me the importance of the values of peace, justice, and love for the sake of the Kingdom. I am grateful for his presence in my own life.

B. Iris, a nurse and educator, draws together a story of a series of mentors who have helped mold her Christian life.

My experience of mentoring involves two distinct and separate circumstances—separate, yet not isolated, as one has blended with and added to the other. In fact, I often find, when I am reflecting upon them, that it is not always possible to identify which is which.

The first experience was with a young priest who was only twenty-eight at the time. I was thirty-nine. It was through his guidance that I began to truly open myself up to a *personal relationship* with the Lord.

During this time I took a major step in the process of self-awareness and healthy self-esteem. This relationship showed me something of the tremendous power that lies in spiritual relationships and sharing, and how sensitivity toward one another's lives can broaden.

This relationship lasted for two years. Letting go was painful and I was uncertain as to whether or not I would want to begin another such relationship. Well—as the Lord would have it, about a year later I met Father Fergus. He was older—about fifty-five. Many things made it clear to me that this was of God's choosing and not mine. This relationshp has been growing for about five years now. Fergus has supported my deepening self-confidence, both in my use of abilities and in my appreciation for the presence of God in various aspects of my life. Fergus has also gently guided me to look deeply at some painful areas of my life and to value them not as failures, but as occasions of grace and greater growth in strength and faith.

The first mentor experience was one of growth in self-love, and the second was one of growth in awareness of the gift of who we are to one another. Each experience enriched and built upon the other. I know that each has been God's way of calling me to wholeness.

C. Lucy, a woman of fifty, relates her story of personal conversion.

I had begun to experience a call to personal holiness and thought my only need was to find someone who would chart the way, i.e., provide me with a program. Ha! During this tryingly beautiful time (which I refer to as that period of life when I was going around knocking on confessional doors) I would regularly and purposely choose a different priest each time I went to confession hoping to find one who did more than absolve sins. A number of priests I sought out in the confessional did not understand the degree of seriousness in my requests for help to grow in perfection. I later came to understand that, for some of them, it was a knowledge of their own limitations that prompted their haste to close the screen as soon as possible. Tear-stained altar rails on a number of Saturday afternoons bore the signs of my inner sorrow. I was disappointed. These priests didn't have the vision to perceive my agony for putting into practice the virtues about which they had spoken so earnestly every Sunday morning.

And then came the memorable occasion when, after confessing, I expressed my real desire to know how to become holy. The priest told me I needed a spiritual director. I had not been familiar with the term. At my request, he agreed to attempt to fulfill that role for me. Here are a few comments regarding my relationship with the person whom I refer to as my mentor:

1. I will never cease to thank God for the gift of direction through this priest.

2. I truly felt that he was being led by the Lord in giving me guidance.

3. While I feel he knew me quite well, he steadfastly refused to make judgments or decisions for me.

4. His familiarity with Scripture opened up for me the wealth of treasure in the Word. He most often prescribed a particular (and startlingly relevant) Scripture verse for a penance.

5. Three words which for me have always been synonymous with his role are:
   a. Sounding-board: Bounce it off me.
   b. Excelsior: To stand still is to fall back.
   c. Cheerleader: You can do it. Give it a try.

6. After these many years, his name and personal intentions are held up by me before the Lord.

7. And, in conclusion, whatever his limitations have been, I'm thankful for his willingness to care enough to always be there, for his continued support and encouragement, for the unquestionable trust in his confidentiality, and for his ability to allow me to comfortably share both my own despicable semblances of pride and the details of an intimate personal relationship with God.

D. Fred, a man in his late fifties and an early retiree from a top executive position, relates to the chairman of the board of a large corporation as his mentor.

Thomas' credo was family, country and company in that order. His dedication to ethics and morality impressed me. I was twenty-six at the time and he was sixty-nine. His morality was the "do unto others" concept, and he lived spiritually a life dedicated to family, country and company. His "people" motivation and sincerity in dealing with day to day problems highlighted the importance of the individual, personal identity, and value. He was always a message of faith in God and self, never capitalizing on weaknesses of others but rather depending on their God-given strengths and talents. He lived the Gospel in business, home and inter-personal relationships.

E. Giles, a man in his late forties, recounts his difficulty defining mentors in his life, although he singles out those who have touched him, including Eleanor, his wife.

> I cannot think of anyone whom I would identify as a spiritual mentor. My spiritual growth has been a series of steps or stages initiated by a person or occurrence, neither of which remained with me to the outcome or to provide me continuous guidance.
>
> Other than Eleanor, no one I can remember has assisted or guided me through any of my periods of growth. My growth has been complemented and accelerated by Eleanor, and in many cases supporting her activities has carried me through dead spots and motivated me to continue in my Christian development.

F. Jim, a priest of fifteen years, writes:

> I appreciate what you are doing in this project. It is valuable. In my life there have been several influential people in terms of vocation, spirituality, intellectual and philosophical growth. I find it difficult to isolate any one of them and tell a story. In many ways I am an eclectic person who has drawn upon the inspiration coming from several sources, all of whom contribute to my self-consciousness and set of values.

G. In her late forties, Patricia describes how she was influenced by three different people as mentors.

> Frank turned around my pollyanna, fairy tale religion. He showed me how to take a stand as an individual without losing or compromising my faith or my beliefs. He exemplified physical and spiritual perseverance and courage. He accomplished through prayer, meditation and professional guidance the ability to make monumental life deci-

sions and to make those decisions with the certainty that God's will was accomplished.

Frank helped me grow into a new dimension of faith by provoking thought without imposing opinions.

Jacqueline is the most prayerful person I know. Her submissiveness to God's will and willingness to allow God to be the master planner in her life has always pointed out to me how far I had to go in letting God be the central core in my own life. From her example I receive encouragement and motivation to keep striving to improve my own prayer life and to surrender my will into the hands of my Creator. This is very hard for me to do—to let go. I am a lot more comfortable in my struggle to let his will happen in my life because of her.

Jacqueline also has a working knowledge of the faith that she shares with others. Her willingness to give of herself, her time and her talent is boundless. She has been a teacher to me, not only in the content of my faith, but in the practice and spreading of it. Knowing her and working with her is a definite plus in working out my own salvation.

Michael presently is my spiritual mentor. He adds depth and dimension to my life in a holistic manner. As a philosopher, he creates for me a system to live by that is realistic and geared to spiritual growth. As a priest, the celebration of eucharistic liturgy with Michael as presiding minister makes up the most important and meaningful part of my week. As a homilist, his thoughts are provocative, carefully planned and relevant to today's society. For me they are excellent sources for adult education. As a teacher, he is a very knowledgeable person and has an incredible ability to transmit this knowledge to others. Through attendance in his classes and in ordinary conversation he inspires me to a higher level of reasoning and lets me know with my mind, what I feel in my heart. As a friend, he accepts me for what I am, allowing me to make mistakes while encouraging me to go on from there in my growth to being a better person. We share common interests in a relationship that is comfortable and acceptable to me. Michael supports me in my endeavors as I am supportive of him in his.

H. Julia, a woman religious for thirty years, describes her relationship with a parish priest.

Twelve years ago, after eighteen years of teaching, I began work in religious education. In my new ministry I met a priest with whom I shared and worked occasionally. I was thirty-eight at the time and John was thirty-four.

After several months in my new work I began to become aware for the first time of some of my gifts. John was very observant. He helped me realize that I had gifts and talents that had not been used. Another great discovery that was made during these months through John's help was to come to the realization that I was loved by others—or, better still, that I could allow others to love me. It is interesting, too, that it was at this time that I began to realize God's great love and care for me, and as a result I learned to appreciate the Scripture saying: "I have called you by your name; you are mine."

John spent time each week with me reflecting on where I was in my relationship with the Lord, how I listened to his word in my life and how I responded to this word as it was lived out each day. As the image of the Lord became clearer and deeper, my relationship with others took on new meaning and became less threatening. John helped me to realize that this was possible only because my own self-image was more secure.

John's concern has opened new vistas for me. His honest yet simple approach has led me to search, reflect, pray and respond to people and the events of everyday life with greater faith and maturity. His patient understanding and support has given me strength, but, most of all, his own deep faith, conviction and commitment has been a constant source of inspiration to me as well as a challenge as I continue to live out my own faith-life and commitment.

I. Ruth recalls when she was twenty-one and in postulancy. Her mentor was forty-five and the postulant mistress.

Since I was embarking on what was to be a life-commitment as a religious sister I cannot think of anyone who had greater influence on my life humanly and spiritually than Sister Myles.

Moving from an affectionate, loving family and an independent life-style into a disciplined convent way of life was made easy by her. She was one of those firm but kind persons whose love, concern, wisdom, understanding and tremendous sense of humor made you feel you were *home*. Because of her deep faith in God grounded in Scripture and love for the Mass I knew that I had someone very special, a model that prompted me to pray each day, "Lord, help me to be just like Sister Myles."

Scripture and individual characters came alive. It was easy to identify with the impulsiveness of St. Peter, the strength of St. Paul, the weakness of Mary Magdalene, and the doubts of doubting Thomas. Her love for the Mass and her theological perspective of it placed her way ahead of her times. Often I hear myself saying, "Sister Myles taught us that forty years ago."

J. Louise looks back at her childhood and adulthood and finds two people who touched her life: her mother and a parish director of religious education.

The first and most outstanding spiritual mentor in my life was my own mother—early memories recall her sincere, strong, simplistic faith. This coupled with that of my family and friends, reinforced by parish priests and sisters, laid the foundation for a solid faith background.

But my spiritual life took a turn several years ago. The changes in the Church through Vatican II overwhelmed and confused me. At the same time a need arose for faithful, practicing Catholic laypersons to assist priests and sisters in teaching religion to children. Along with others, I was called upon for this role. Programs to prepare adults to teach were offered—classes in Scripture, Church, sacraments, liturgy and music provided us with a deeper knowledge and understanding of Christ and his love for us.

These programs and the direction, support and concern offered by our director enabled me to grow spiritually from elementary to adult level in faith. This spiritual mentor, along with other priests, teachers, lecturers, reinforced my faith at a time when it was needed most. The awesome feeling and the realization that Christ loves us despite our weaknesses and human frailties awakened an awareness in my spiritual life and provided growth in knowledge and love of God, and the ability to teach these gifts to others—a new dimension to *my* faith.

THE SHORTCOMINGS IN SPIRITUAL MENTORING

All human events have shortcomings. Although blessed by the Spirit Christian mentoring is no less subject to the inadequacies of human nature. We should keep in mind that adult mentoring works, but not all the time. When it does, we thank God; when it doesn't, we are grateful for the gift of humility.

It is important that those who become mentors in formal parish programs or who administrate these programs be well advised of the limitations of mentoring. This is especially pertinent in the adult catechumenate wherein the sponsor-mentor assumes a significant and public role. At times it may be reasonable to draw up a distinct job description for formal parish roles so that expectations may be realizable and reasonable. Further suggestions about mentors which can benefit the sponsor role in the adult catechumenate can be found in Chapters IV and V.

There are four shortcomings to be considered in the mentoring process. They are offered here not so much to warn us off as to invite comment and to help us understand ourselves.

The Human Factor

Many may presently be mentors in our lives, although they might not even know it. Human pride often keeps the novice from giving any clue to the mentor. If someone does not share the need for mentorship or doesn't know how to, mentors are bereft of the knowledge needed to refine their gifts.

Even when mentors have come to recognize their mentoring role, the process may become tedious and long. Novices often need more from mentors than mentors can give. And the emotional drain may be exhausting. Knowing when to draw the line between mentor and novice is a skill learned but never easily exercised.

The Ecclesial Factor

Those involved in Christian mentoring are involved in Church work. And so there will be demands made, containment required, expectations laid out. Because spiritual mentoring often happens in an ecclesial format, mentors serve the collective body of the Church and will be disciplined by its norms. In some cases mentoring may be prohibited either because it threatens some roles or because it does not fit bureaucratic lines. In other cases money, structures and laziness will get in the way.

There will never be a time when all these disturbing elements are eliminated. Mentors have to learn to work within limitations and, if they can change them, to do so.

The Personal Factor

The most difficult area to deal with is the novice's choice not to have a mentor. I would remind all of us of St. Mark's Gospel (Mk 10:17–22) where Jesus offers the rich young man the chance for a mentor-novice relationship, and the offer is rejected. Adults will be adults, making decisions for better or worse. Many may need mentoring but many will refuse it precisely because they are afraid of change, have been taught to avoid risk or cannot pull themselves out of a spiritual rut. The Christian adult mentor has only one refuge in this kind of situation—prayer.

The Novice Factor

Mentors have feelings too. Give a large portion of your life to aid another person and you expect some return.

The Christian mentor must realize that the novice will eventually move on, no longer needing the mentor. This is the way it should be.

Becoming too emotionally attached to the novice is not good. Try keeping an emotional distance that will allow the novice to become a mentor too.

When the novice no longer needs the mentor, the mentor has done a good job.

The ex-novice's task is to prove the worth of mentoring by how the Christian life is lived.

The function of the Christian mentor seems relevant to our present age. In light of the fact that we have a story to tell—a liberating and reconciling one—we are called to provide the means applicable to our age, rendering it anew. The mentor is a concept which may be helpful to the Christian community. It should be investigated and experimented with. Walking with the Lord has always been the grand experiment that has captured our imaginations. Perhaps we should do more walking together.

WHAT CAN SPIRITUAL MENTORS DO FOR US?

Spiritual mentors can help us face what Michael Crosby in *The Spirituality of the Beatitudes* calls the circle of insight. A spiritual mentor helps us move from those experiences which jar our world and our complacency into a new worldview and consciousness. Having disturbing experiences falls to the lot of us. However, these experiences will often fall to naught if they are not channeled into a new consciousness making us more uncertain but much wiser about life.

Spiritual mentors can also support us in learning to live without having to be the center of the universe. The transition from young adulthood to adulthood confronts the individual with the uneasy thought that others have been here before us and already have answers many times more adequate than our own. Finding support while going through a difficult passage helps us grow in respect for each other.

Spiritual mentors can aid us in combating the quagmire of consumerism: that hellish whirlpool of advertising gimmickry which objectifies and dehumanizes us. Through mentors we can begin to see that we are more than we eat/drink/buy. We are loved by a God who has made us complete in himself.

Spiritual mentors can assist us in coming to terms with God's Kingdom. Eventually appreciating that God's Kingdom is less about what we've done and more about who we have become, we learn to move gently with the Lord.

Spiritual mentors can challenge us to be open to God's grace in ourselves and in others. God's grace purifies and moves us to grow beyond where we are.

Mentors who assist our spiritual lives can enable us to share our substance with those who lack those elements necessary for life. If we are chastised for our constant need to consume the earth's goods while others die for lack of daily needs, we have been correctly awakened to our responsibility for each other.

A spiritual mentor is to prod us to embrace the deserts of our souls and the fertile valleys of our faith. Appreciating that our life's journey may combine both, we are more sensitized to the power of God over the power of evil.

Lastly, spiritual mentors can provide us with cause to hope in God's ultimate victory where sin, sickness and death will be no more.

CHANGE, DEVELOPMENT AND DEPENDENCE

Evelyn Underhill in *Practical Mysticism* claims that the mystical resurrects in our lives as transitions bring us more and more away from the safe and secure and into a new land. It is at this moment of transition that we are the weakest, for the temptation is to stay put and not to move on. But we will change despite our reluctance. Thankfully others who have faced change successfully are waiting to walk with us.

Erik Erikson whose theories of personal development underlie many modern approaches to life advocates autonomy as the successful engagement with life. But Erikson's goal of authentic autonomy may run contrary to the process of transition, especially in the Christian sense. The older we get the more we become dependent on our environment and relationships, not the contrary. If Erikson implies his ideal of autonomy during the years of young adulthood there is much credit to establishing separation here. But after that point in life limits begin to be imposed on us which sooner or later we must succumb to—and redefine our independence in terms of interdependence and community.

Recall that Erikson draws his ladder of development from Freudian psychology and in a male-dominated culture—a culture grounded in separation and individuation rather than subjectivity and attachment.

Nevertheless, as in Francis Thompson's classic poem, God chases us down the corridors of life hard on our heels to have us hold him near and dear.

Examples of increased dependence on God, i.e., giving up on selfism and opting for other-centeredness, are seen in men like Jonah, and Sts. Paul, Peter and Thomas More. Initially each fights against the emotional and feminine need to trust in the Lord, trying to duck it by working it out in a competitive-analytical model of life.

MALE, FEMALE AND BONDING

Interestingly when one stands back from the male-dominated model of life we find females more adept at lifetime dependent maturing, as well as deeper moral insightfulness (Carol Gilligan, *In a Different Voice*). Differences in perceptions of intimate relationships are demonstrated by Gilligan's control groups as closeness evokes violence in many males and separateness conjures up the same in females. History shows that culture influences and conditions sex-role types. Men as a composite group seem to shy away from group dependence, therapy and intimacy because they perceive this as unmasculine, weak and too emotional. However, as Levinson reports, when males find mentoring groups or persons with whom safe commonality can be established and the emotive, intuitive life affirmed, they encounter great difficulty breaking away from that new-found intimacy.

Consequently when this bonding occurs between mentor and novice there is formed not only a pseudo-symbiotic union but a handicap as well. Growth beyond transitional needs may be stymied by such closeness. It should be presumed that the mentor-novice community should lead to a separation which thrusts the novice into new bonding and a sharper definition of one's life. In breaking from the mentor, after a successful relationship, the novice re-forms community (attachment in the Eriksonian sense) with others-than-the-mentor. This is as it should be.

One could venture that the subsequent transition to a fuller life can culminate in an androgynous synthesis where both feminine and masculine sides of the personality (in the Jungian sense) are harmonized.

IMAGES

Ann Ulanov in *The Feminine in Theology and Psychology* describes the symbolism in transition as a means to spiritual insightfulness. In understanding our images of God and ourselves, and inasmuch as our mentors are able to help us integrate these images, no matter how crude or powerful, we come to terms with the person-we-are-becoming. The result? A holistic appreciation that who-I-am-to-become is connected to the One-to-whom-I-return.

A mentor assists the development of our spiritual life by insisting that we confront our images of God, life and destiny which have served one or more phases of life, but now need to be re-examined. In this way we may pass from the desert of our experiences to the fruitfulness of the Spirit. However this transition happens within the context of our unique personal story. Paraphrasing Anne Sexton, we are given one hand to play at life, and only that hand; it is ours to use and use wisely.

There are times, Eugene Bianchi notes in *Aging as a Spiritual Journey*, when the signs of change, physical and spiritual, bring us closer to nature, friends, body, time and peace. These movements are more than metabolic clues to the ebb and flow of our bodily shifts. They signal the ripening of life—times for questioning images about growing more mature, becoming one with the one-we-are-to-become.

SYNTHESIS

The synthesis which I cannot help but draw from research and the expressions of others is: spiritual mentorship is more the result of infused giftedness and less of a learned technique. If one fact is repeated over and over again by people who affirm significant mentors in their lives, it is that these mentors knew how to listen and waited patiently for their novice's response. There is a God-given fullness in the spiritual mentor which must be spilled out for others. Indeed this poignant message is the essence of a parable of Jesus found in St. Luke's Gospel (Lk 13:18–19) about the mustard seed. The smallest start explodes into the greatest finish.

MOVING ON

In this chapter we investigated the role of a Christian mentor. We examined the functions and shared people's stories about mentors. In the following chapter our attention will turn to finding spiritual mentors. We will investigate how we perceive ourselves and our expectations. By gaining deeper insights into ourselves we will describe our need for mentors, suggesting how to use them as spiritual energies.

IV.

Finding Spiritual Mentors

After days spent in classifying stories about significant spiritual mentors, I received a letter from Bob Metcalf with a different sort of story. Somehow Bob had found out that I was surveying people's stories about spiritual mentors. And so he wrote me describing his spiritual experiences—none of which could adequately be described here as stories about spiritual mentors.

But Bob had to tell me his experiences, assuming that I would be a good listener. Metcalf is thirty-seven years old and overwhelmed that his life is going through an upheaval. Social scientists would understand his struggle as late young adult emerging into middle adult transition. I was tempted to discard his correspondence as irrelevant and uninvited. But as I reread his account I wondered whether his story might not be the reason why people need mentors.

Bob Metalf is undergoing transition. Recall that one premise in this study has been that transitions need sponsoring. For lack of any better definition Bob's personal account was one of personal struggle without benefit of mentor support. No one was walking with him.

Experiences often package needs. Consider the best and worst moments of life. Did they come about spontaneously without reason or were they the result of an increasing awareness of needs in life—needs so deep that relationships and vocation were changed in the resolution?

Our experiences are oftentimes the descriptions of our needs. Does our heart ache because of lost love? Do our futures evaporate because of missed chances? Could it be that experiences are negatively aggravated by unspoken needs—needs so deep, so personal that we may be unable to verbalize them?

If life generally is directed by needs, these also touch our spirituality. Some claim that maturity brings out inner transcendent needs. If this is true, and I have no reason to doubt its authenticity, then as we address our spiritual experiences we address our spiritual needs.

Many of us, and Bob Metcalf was a timely example, are returnees to the spiritual life. The old maxim of "sowing our wild oats" is not far from the reality of our lives. Age may not be a fair criterion by which to judge this phase. I've known men and women in their fifties who were no more settled or mature in their lifestyles than those thirty years their juniors. But we do act unwisely at times. We often misjudge situations by the absence of value and lack of experiences in our lives. Eventually spiritual questions do arise. And when they do, new answers are needed. Seeking to illuminate our darkened way, we look for someone who can provide the light. Mentors are on fire with experience. Catching the fire from them, we can reilluminate our paths.

WHAT TO LOOK FOR IN SPIRITUAL MENTORS

Throughout this book we have suggested that there are roles and functions appropriate to spiritual mentors. We have looked at the mentor from the mentor's vantage point.

If we direct ourselves to our needs and the experiences of transition we must view the mentor from this focus. The questions that flow from this bias are: When one is struggling with change what kind of mentor fits the need best? How does one get to know apt mentors? Can one recognize those pertinent qualities in a person which will assure some reliability?

I believe we can distinguish those who can be good mentors from those who cannot. A spiritual mentor is one who has utilized God's gifts in life. Good mentors are sensitive to their historical and social roles. Unencumbered by false humility they move easily with the fact that God has gifted them with special talents. They prize these talents and can share them. Inasmuch as mentors recognize and love their own gifts, they can help us love ours.

A spiritual mentor is one who appreciates silence, especially inner silence. If one is uncomfortable with one's own pain, unable to accept the struggle of introspective reflection, one cannot listen to another's pleadings. Discipline is a *sine qua non* quality in a mentor. Trained to replenish themselves by silence, good spiritual mentors commune with God's spirit. Their sensitivity to their own needs helps them direct their energies on our behalf.

Spiritual mentors must be people at home with prayer. A spiritual mentor is to be known for a prayer-filled life. Obviously if one cannot converse with God one cannot converse with God's creatures.

Spiritual mentors are searchers. In constant quest of holiness, the mentor illustrates a life bent on bringing the human spirit in harmony with God's spirit. Mentors who exhibit no tendency to be holy are to be avoided.

Consequently, the mentors who reverence silence, prayer and the ongoing quest for holiness are the ones who love God's creation. Awed by God's great work wrought in the universe, a spiritual mentor reverences God's power. And as God's creation we receive both affirmation and blessings from a spiritual mentor.

Spiritual mentors value trust, the quality of human relationships. A good spiritual mentor will trust us because trust has been found first of all in God. Trust a spiritual mentor and the relationship will prove what love means.

Those committed to spiritual mentorship know what struggle and failure mean. Without having seen strife, having missed the buffets of misfortune, a mentor would be an empty sign. Bruised but healed, a spiritual mentor prizes the inequities of life as symbolic of crucifixion. As with the good thief who is taken with Jesus into happy holiness, spiritual mentors can help us find solace because they have been there too.

Wisely enough spiritual mentors aid our spiritual passage when they help us confront the un-Christian values in our lives—in the world. There is a prophetic nuance to spiritual mentoring. One person's pain is everyone's pain. A mentor opens up to us the possibility of telling the difference between good and bad spirits.

Those whom we should choose as spiritual mentors are not fooled by the world's values. They are also not bewitched by cheap grace. Spiritual maturing comes through hard work. Mentors will illustrate for us what empowerment in real grace, God's spirit at work, really means.

In short those to whom we can look for credible wisdom are those who have the fire of the Spirit in their lives. We would do well to catch any spark that flies our way.

ENERGIZED BY THE SPIRITUAL JOURNEY

Lorraine at twenty-seven had hit a crisis point. She needed new energy. Her story follows.

I had begun to recognize the need to examine my faith as an adult. My high school understanding of it was no longer appropriate. I also began to consider changing my occupation. This meant walking away from something I had been doing for eight years, returning to school, and then starting all over again.

During this time, as well as many other times in the past five years, I have gone to Vinnie when I've found myself in the midst of a struggle. I have done so with the feeling that he understands and can relate to what I am experiencing.

At first I looked to him for answers. But I learned early along that I'd only get more questions. He would say what I didn't want but needed to hear. I now value this because with Vinnie I am able to get right to the heart of the matter, and am able to more honestly appraise the effect each situation has upon my relationship with myself, God, and others. Vinnie gives me new energy.

We are reminded by a popular TV commercial that life can be energized. The energy needed here is not the product of consumerist hype but the living power that comes to us from living sources. Lorraine described her spiritual mentor in energy terms. For her Vinnie was more than an astute listener. He was also a vital, challenging individual who drew out of her new insights, new power. Vinnie didn't give Lorraine new power—though her words could convey that sense. He helped her draw it from herself and God.

We are aroused to a new concern, challenged into action when our mentors help us tap hidden resources in our own inner spirit.

The main source of our spiritual energy is in the Spirit of God. The Spirit continues to generate positive pressures in us, God's grace, and we in turn are to use it for championing life. For many, these powers lay dormant for years. It takes an awakening to revitalize and use them. Part of this utilization comes with our maturation, through our transitions. Like struggling mountain climbers we must reach out to our ropes to give us leverage.

Energizers are those people, like mentors, who can touch our lives in ways which unleash our special powers. Once the power is released we are changed by the force of its possibilities.

Energizers can be our peers who need us to support them in their own struggle. Because our travails are similar we unleash in each other the power needed to sustain momentum.

Energizers may be our friends. Intimate associates know how to touch us. Where closed to others, friends know where to strike a nerve, opening up a torrent of power. If we accept their challenge we may actualize our God-given talent—talent which otherwise might have gone stale.

Fellow believers can help us get up steam. Together common endeavors support our decision making and we move because we have confidence in that fidelity.

God by his grace is the prime initiator. Creator of all things living, God provides us with hidden powers in our lives as well as those who can help us tap them.

IN CONCLUSION

After all these thoughts, a story shared by Marcel has the earmarks of closure.

> Phil taught me by example what a biblical Christian truly was, i.e., a faith which moves the love and study of the Scriptures into daily life. Furthermore, his zeal for his work, and his enthusiasm for the ministry gave me something to aim for. He treated me as a student, and a friend, and opened for me the door to adult living by his support and his challenges.

Taking the theories about life and directing them into the practical means for living are the results of good spiritual mentoring.

The task of this chapter, as we stated at the very beginning, was to underscore the needs of adults to find spiritual mentors. The results of the survey proved over and over again that adults who have found spiritual mentors have found themselves as well as the strength to weather the process of life.

From the beginning our premise has been that transitions need sponsoring. All the more evident is that people need sponsoring to engage fruitfully in the process of their changing lives.

The conclusions which we can draw from our reflections are the sum total of our life expectations: (1) We are loved and need to be loved to survive. (2) We can love and by loving do survive. (3) We are changing and in our changes can become who we should be. (4) We are changed by those with whom we live. (5) We change those with whom we live. (6) Some of us can be spiritual guides. (7) These talents do not alleviate the pain of life; rather these talents support us as we weather that pain. (8) We become mentors ourselves when we are open to having mentors ourselves. (9) God works through us to bring us back to himself. (10) As we recognize him as our destiny, we learn what being human is all about.

People like ourselves are the subjects of mentoring. People like ourselves are the mentors yet-to-come from the mentors already there. We are therefore each other's keepers.

My conclusions and ideas about spiritual mentors were shared with participants at a New England symposium of adult religious educators. The feedback was affirming and engaging. Based on that response I have drawn together the next and final chapter, collating the reflections based on this exchange.

V.

Reflections

Rose, a married woman of sixty, reflects on her Christian faith and leaves us with this story.

When I was about twenty years old and my younger child became ill, I desperately needed someone to encourage me. My mother had always been there but at that time I needed someone not so emotionally involved.

In the neighborhood was a person who belonged to the Christian Missionary Alliance Church. She was a loving and concerned soul. She prayed with me and I began to go to their Bible study groups in her home. I also went to her church.

A friend in the neighborhood who was Catholic encouraged me to see Father Joe. I told him about my struggle and he asked me how much I knew about the Catholic religion. I told him I knew what I had been taught in the Baltimore Catechism but that was behind me. He suggested I take a home study course. He would serve as my guide.

His words and prayers were so encouraging. I stopped going to the other church. Now I knew that being a Catholic was a gift. I began to appreciate it more and more. I saw him regularly.

The Catholic Action census was being taken that year. I don't know why I signed a card saying that I would help. I had not been involved before in the Church. The night that the orientation meeting was held, I decided not to attend. The phone rang and it was the new priest Father Bill from the parish. He asked me if I was coming to the meeting. I answered: "Do you really need me?" His reply was: "Everyone is needed." I know that the voice I heard on the phone that night was really the Holy Sprit.

Father began a class for people who were not Catholic and I went along with a friend. I planned to go only once but it stretched out for several years. It was there that I began to take my spiritual life seriously.

I could not get enough to satisfy the spiritual hunger I felt. I read spiritual books constantly. Nothing else mattered. Father guided me to the life of prayer and daily Communion.

Father Bill gave me a purpose for living and joy of prayer. I believe that the Holy Spirit was instrumental in having him as my spiritual mentor. I had done nothing to merit this wonderful friend. I thank God for his friendship and understanding.

BEING CATHOLIC

Rose's story illustrates the point of this whole book: transitions need sponsoring. At least three mentors helped her find meaning and community in the faith.

We must draw some reflections on all that has been said, and these must inevitably say something about being Catholic. There is no intention here to say that other Christians might not have the same experiences. But it suffices for us to identify that specific community and heritage pertinent to many Catholic Christians.

Recall that mentors respond to their gift of sponsorhip by catching others on fire with who they are to be. A Christian mentor specifies this—bringing a novice into communion with the Lord Jesus. A Catholic mentor directs the novice into the Catholic experience.

What specifically Catholic elements can a mentor illustrate for a novice? Five elements come to mind. Each describes the experience of being Catholic.

Sacramentality: the Catholic experience of Christianity is not about seven sacraments but about celebrating the key moments of human life informed through divine intervention and advocacy. A Catholic mentor draws the novice into the context of being Catholic. That context illustrates in seven ways how the Lord Jesus and his spirit radically motivate Catholic life. The novice gains entrance into Catholic spirituality by grabbing hold of these seven keys opening up a treasury of Catholic experiences.

Heritage: the Catholic mentor helps the novice establish limits. Limits in the Catholic sense are the rituals and social standards which guide the community to its identity as Catholic. A novice comes to the awareness that faith is circumscribed by social identification: faith like life gets contained by the world events surrounding our lives. The novice ultimately learns that heritage is more than one's memory system. It is much more—it is the collective memory of a believing community.

Faith Issues: a Catholic mentor leads the novice slowly into the house of Catholic truths. The mentor attempts to unfold for the novice the treasure of doctrine and revelation entrusted to the living, believing and destined community. The novice comes to the conclusion that one is invited into a living creed—one which says as much about the Church as it does about the individual believer.

Life Affirming: Christianity has been described many ways. A singularly keen observation would isolate the concept of hope. A Catholic mentor opens up the novice to a hope-filled destiny. Catholic life always looks toward transformation, renewal and resurrection. The mentor is to aid the novice in finding this meaning for life.

Family: being Catholic is being bonded—belonging to a community entrusted with propagating a message of justice, trust, intimacy and love. The novice becomes bonded to the body of Christ through the insights of the mentor. The novice will hopefully draw the conclusions that the Catholic family is as strong and enduring as a personal one.

FINDING GOD

Lois recalls with warmth a special relationship with her aunt.

Aunt Ruth had always been friend, confidante, relative and spiritual guide. She guided me growing up by sharing and listening. When my parents did not seem to understand me or were impatient with me she always understood. Her faith and joy have been an inspiration to me. Although tragedy filled her life, her strength, trust and love of God manifested itself. Just her presence provided me with stability. There is no doubt that in having Ruth in my life I have had God.

Having God in one's life is no mean accomplishment. When the novice comes to realize that the mentor's greatest accomplishment is in the novice's awareness of God, the novice has entered a new phase of living.

After all, life for the believing person is a process of disclosure. We find out more about who we are to be in discovering the God who is. And we perceive God's presence in those who have been given to us as God's gifts—our mentors.

CELEBRATING OUR HUMANNESS

Human nature at its best is celebration. If we could somehow collate our funerals and weddings, making them into a constant event of life, we would become more aware of how much our coming and going are the real stories of living. But we can't. And so we must sustain ourselves on a glimpse of what being human means (through the lenses of suffering—sorrow, healing, joy). The flame which keeps burning brightly in us sustains the means for holding onto the essences of life. Catching that fire comes through each of us—each in time being mentor and novice to one another. Each catching and holding dear the fire that glimmers in our eyes.

Tom's story will sustain all that has been said.

When I was twenty-five and studying for my M.S.W. I found employment with the Public Welfare Department in New York. There I was put under the tutelage of the unit supervisor Solomon Citron, fifty-four and a fervent Jew.

Solomon was a bachelor who cared for his aged parents while saving to send his younger brothers to medical school. Solomon was the nearest thing to Jesus Christ I had ever met.

His life was the epitome of patience, understanding, wisdom, kindness and endurance. His life taught me the beauty of humanity, broad-mindedness, and empathy. A modest man, it was only by accident that I learned of his charity to the poor and encouragement of workers. In fact his humility was contagious.

Solomon taught me how to live without rash judgments, with love and sacredness for my work. A renewed spirituality developed in me—he touched me to the core of my being, not with himself but with his love for the Other. His affirmation of life made the human holy. I was made holy, alive for the Lord.

Resources

Bianchi, Eugene. *Aging as a Spiritual Journey.* New York: Crossroads, 1982.

Bolton, E. "A Conceptual Analysis of the Mentor Relationship in the Career Development of Women." *Adult Education,* 1980, 30, 195–207.

Boston, B.O. *The Sorcerer's Apprentice: A Case Study in the Role of the Mentor.* 1976. (ERIC Document Reproduction Service No. Ed. 126–671).

Boyack, Kenneth. *A Parish Guide to Adult Initiation.* Ramsey, New Jersey: Paulist Press, 1980.

Burton, A. "The Mentoring Dynamic in the Therapeutic Transformation." *American Journal of Psychoanalysis,* 1977, 37, 115–122.

Callino, E. G. C. and Scott, P. (eds.), "Everyone Who Makes It Has a Mentor." *Harvard Business Review,* 1978, 89–101.

Conway, Jim. *Men in Mid Life Crisis.* Elgin, Illinois: David C. Cook, 1978.

Crosby, Michael. *The Spirituality of the Beatitudes.* Maryknoll, New York: Orbis Books, 1981.

Dujarier, Michel. *The Rites of Christian Initiation,* trans. by Kevin Hart. New York: Sadlier, 1979.

Dunning, James. *New Wine in New Wineskins.* New York: Sadlier, 1981.

Edwards, Tilden. *Sabbath Time.* New York: Seabury Press, 1982.

———. *Spiritual Friend.* Ramsey, New Jersey: Paulist Press, 1980.

Erickson, K. and Pitner, N.J. "The Mentor Concept Is Alive and Well." *NASSP Bulletin,* 1980, 64, 8–13.

Erikson, Erik. *Childhood and Society.* New York: Norton, 1950.

Gilligan, Carol. *In a Different Voice.* Boston: Harvard Univ. Press, 1981.

Greeley, Andrew. *The Religious Imagination.* New York: Sadlier, 1981.

Groome, Thomas. *Christian Religious Education.* San Francisco: Harper and Row, 1980.

Hoge, Dean. *Converts, Dropouts and Returnees.* USCC, Washington, and New York: Pilgrim Press, 1981.

Kemp, Raymond. *A Journey in Faith.* New York: Sadlier, 1979.

Levinson, Daniel, *et al., The Seasons of a Man's Life.* New York: Ballantine Books, 1979.

May, Gerald. *Care of Mind, Care of Spirit.* San Francisco: Harper and Row, 1982.

Merriam, S. "Mentors and Protégés: A Critical Review of the Literature." *Adult Education.* Vol. 33, No. 3, Spring 1983, pp. 161–173.

Metz, Johann Baptist. *Faith in History and Society,* trans. by David Smith. New York: Seabury, 1980.

O'Collins, Gerald. *The Second Journey.* Ramsey, New Jersey: Paulist Press, 1978.

———. *Rite of Christian Initiation of Adults.* provisional text, USCC, Washington, D.C., 1974.

Shapiro, E. C., Haseltine, F., and Row, M. "Moving Up: Role Models, Mentors and The Patron System." *Sloan Management Review,* 1978, 19, 51–58.

Shea, John. "Storytelling and Religious Identity." *Chicago Studies.* Vol. 21, No 1, Spring 1982, pp. 23–43.

———. *Stories of Faith.* Chicago: Thomas More Press, 1980.

Sheehy, G. "The Mentor Connection: The Secret Link in the Successful Woman's Life." *New York Magazine,* April 5, 1976, pp. 33–39.

———. *Pathfinders.* New York: William Morrow, 1981.

Simmons, Henry. "The Quiet Journey: Psychological Development and Religious Growth from Ages Thirty to Sixty." *Religious Education.* Vol. LXXI, No. 2, March–April, 1976, pp. 132–142.

Toffler, Alvin. *Third Wave.* New York: William Morrow, 1980.

Ulanov, Ann. *Receiving Woman: Studies in Theology and Psychology of the Feminine.* Philadelphia: Westminster, 1981.

Underhill, Evelyn. *Mysticism.* New York: Dutton, 1961.

———. *Practical Mysticism.* New York: Dutton, 1960.

Vaillant, G. *Adaptation to Life.* Boston: Little, Brown and Co., 1977.

Weber, C. E. "Mentoring." *Directors and Boards.* Fall 1980, pp. 17–24.